This Book Belongs To:

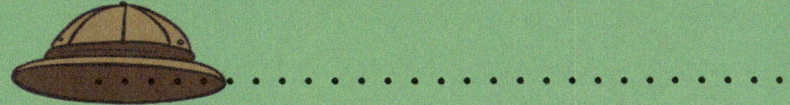

Words and Original
Illustrations by:

Angelina P. Fioretti

Recreated
Illustrations by:

Angelina P. Fioretti
and
Brenda J. Fioretti

Published by:
PiccoloBlumen Books

Copyright © 2019
All Rights Reserved
ISBN 978-1-9990046-0-6 Hardcover
ISBN 978-0-9952979-2-0 Paperback
ISBN 978-1-9990046-1-3 Audio
ISBN 978-0-9952979-2-0 E-book

Acknowledgements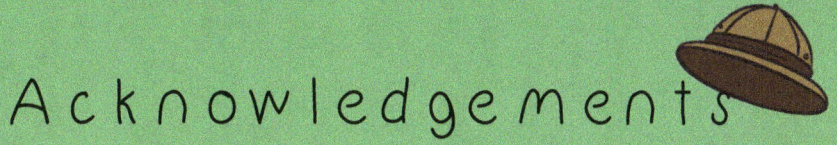

Thank you Dinosaur Train for teaching me science in a fun way.

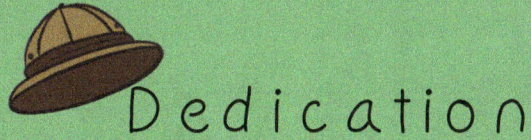 ## Dedication

This book is for other kids who love digging for treasures as much as me.

When I grow up
I will be
an Archaeologist.

I hope it will be fun.

I hope that I
will make friends.

And have a nice boss.

I think that being an
Archaeologist will be fun.

And I like out doors because
it is fun being outside.

I hope I will be happy being an Archaeologist.

And I hope I will be happy being there with my friends.

And with my boss.

And I don't care
if my boss says
I have to do alot of things
at once.

Because I know she is nice.

I hope I will be happy
being an Archaeologist.

And I hope
I will be happy being there
with my friends
and with my boss.

THE END

What do you want to be
when you grow up?

Did you like this book?

Was it good?

If this book inspires someone you know to write a story, spread the word by leaving a review on **amazon** or **ask your local bookstore or librarian to order it!**

Angelina's Original
Story . . .

How I Grow Up

how II grow up.
by Angellna Fioretti

Wen I ero up I will be a reol
I hope it will be fun

I hope theat I will
make felens and have
a nice bos

I think that being an rceoliest will be fun and I like awt dors because it is fun being awtsid.

"I love awt dors"

I hop I will be happy being a rceoligist and I hop I will be happy being that with my frens and my bos.

I dont car if my bos ass that I hf to do alot of things at onre, beracuse I know that she is niss.

"but you hafto"
"but I cant do that..."

Did you lik this store wuz it gud

About the Author

When Angelina was very small one of her favourite things to do was carry a stack of books from her bookshelf to her bed where she would tell her stories aloud. Her love of books came early.

When she started printing she made the letter A into a person by adding a smiley face and hair. These 'A' people, as we called them, found their way into her stories and before we knew it, the *Angelina's An Author Series* was born!

For a school project, Angelina wrote this and two other published stories when she was just six. The illustrations and custom font from her printing were re-created under her guidance. She always wanted to be an author, so why wait? She has stories to share now!

In addition to being an author, Angelina wants to be a gymnastics teacher and archaeologist when she grows up. We have no doubt she will be, and whatever else she dreams up. She lives with her family and her dogs in Alberta, Canada.

If you like this book and love the idea of kids following their dreams, check out Angelina's books and fun stuff at **angelinasanauthor.com.** Tell your local school, bookstore and library about her books!